LOVE LIVES HERE

THE SECRET SAUCE TO A HAPPY RELATIONSHIP

BY

GADIFELE MOENG

ISBN: 978-0-620-91675-2 (Print)

Illustrator: Motsanaphe Morare (MoMaLifeLiving.com)

Editor and Proof-reader: Luyanda Thela
(ldlamini@thegoldengooseinstitute.com)

I would love to hear from you. Your questions and comments are welcome. Don't be a stranger. My contact information is listed below, and I encourage you to contact me. I am also available for speaking engagements.

My email address is gadispeaks@exclusivemail.co.za

This book was published by
The Golden Goose Institute (Pty) Ltd

For further information email:
info@thegoldengooseinstitute.com

CONTENTS

FOREWORD

"The attitude is that of service, the attitude is that of giving and the attitude is that of sacrifice"
– Sarah Jakes Roberts

HOW CAN I SERVE YOU? This is definitely the question that each party to a romantic relationship should be asking their partner—at all times. The intention should be to out-serve your partner at any given opportunity. Gadifele Moeng captures this important aspect of a relationship so well through this amazing book. *Love Lives Here* is a masterpiece. It is so necessary! To say Gadifele loves LOVE is an understatement! She is a true advocate of LOVE and she practices every piece of advice she has documented in this book.

I met Gadifele in 2016, at a Toastmasters meeting, where she was delivering a speech about how she met Mr K—the love of her life. It is such a privilege to witness first-hand the love dance between these two amazing human beings.

What I love about Gadifele, which also permeates throughout this book, is her ability to be candid about both the beautiful and the not-so-pretty side of love and romantic relationships. This book is NOT about the airy-fairy stories about love and romance. It is a useful guide on how to navigate your own relationship and how to personalise your own love journey. More importantly, this book eloquently outlines valuable lessons, as shared by people who have walked their own journeys; successfully so.

I admire how Gadifele managed to capture each couple's love journey, in such a way that it offers much-needed nuggets for the reader. From learning to cover your love partner's shortfalls, to the juicy topic of sex, Gadifele does not shy away from any topic. She shows vulnerability by sharing the mistakes she made in her marriage and the lessons she learned and applied.

Through reading this book, I am inspired to be open to love, to experience my own beautiful love story because "love is not a feeling; love is a decision."

Morongwa Moshole
Mentor, IT Operations Leader and Business Woman

INTRODUCTION

According to Fatherly.com, within the first to the ninth year of marriage, heterosexual couples increase their chances of divorce year on year until they get into their tenth year. I grew up with the idea that I was going to get married. Most ladies are groomed for marriage by family and society as a whole. We would see it in soap operas, romantic comedies, and stories shared by our families.

If most of us have the dream of getting married, then the above statistic may bring a cause of concern to you. It's this cause of concern that has birthed the book that is in your hands.

The motivation for this book is centred on sharing the wisdom of people who have been married for at least ten years. The intention is for you to understand how they have stayed together for that long. I will be sharing stories from seven different couples that have been together for more than ten years and one that ended before that time. Of course, I have to also share something about myself.

I hope that you learn from the mistakes made by some couples in this book and learn from their triumphs as well. In doing so, whether you wish to get married, are getting married, or are in a marriage, you will be well equipped to surf the waves of trials.

For your convenience at the end of every chapter, I have included a section called "The Love Lives Here Idea." I want you to engage with the questions or ideas shared to anchor the message of the chapter.

Enjoy the read and may you and your spouse's lives be better because of it.

Chapter 1

MY JOURNEY TO WRITING THIS BOOK

For the longest of times, relationship dynamics have always fascinated me. The idea behind why some people can stay longer in them while others hardly find a match beats me. I'm interested in understanding who, in a relationship, might be the keeper or who is likely to give up when the going gets tough. Relationships are not always easy-going or rosy. As glamorous as they may look from the outside, one may never know what is brewing inside the pot. They can be a place of happiness where hearts are joined, secrets are shared, and memories are made. They can also be a place of contest, heartbreaks, and sources of regrets. Some people are only glad to come out of them alive.

My fascination drove me to explore relationships. To feed my curiosity, I took the opportunity to interview seven couples who have been together for more than ten years. I also interviewed a divorcee. Ten years is the magic number—the breaking point. The goal was to uncover secrets to successful relationships if any. The first port of call was my relationship with my husband Mr K. I met him sixteen years ago when we both had just moved to Johannesburg. It has not been without its challenges, having been tested so many times. We have managed to always pick up the pieces after a difficult spell. One day I asked him what has made him stay for this long. "It is a choice," he answered. This was not the kind of answer I was looking for. I expected he would say that it was due to his love for me or that I am to die for. Surely, I must have been doing something right for him to stay this long. This cannot be reduced to just a choice. In this case, he means that it is in his hands and that he can change his mind anytime he wishes to. While his answer sounds harsh, in reality, it is true. Most people stay in relationships on their own terms. We think we have control over how we can keep a relationship together when we do not. Do we choose to stay in good or bad relationships?

There are so many theories out there on how to keep a partner. The sharers of these theories may say things like, "He will only stay if you bath at least twice a day" or "If you are not good in bed, he or she is gone." I am not an expert so I cannot confirm nor deny any of this but in the end, I agree with my husband that it is your choice to stay.

In that same breath, however, I understand that the simplicity in that idea is not meant to be the answer for all marriages out there. No solution is a one size fits all. We human beings, whilst created equal, are not the same and do not behave the same way. Some may choose to leave a good partner, and some may choose to stay with a bad partner. As long as it makes sense to them.

The first question I would like you to answer would be – have you made the choice? Have you decided that you will be with your partner through thick and thin, sickness and in health, for richer or poorer?

If the answer is "no" or "it depends," I would ask you to reconsider your decision of getting married. Marriage is like taking your boat out into the ocean. When the waves of trials head your way, you do not leave the boat. You stay in it and navigate the sea waters. Also, remember that I have assumed that you have already seen your partner's character for what it is as opposed to what you would want it to be.

If your answer is a "yes," then l ask that you journey with me page by page, assessing what couples have been saying from the beginning of their marriage to ten years from the date they both said yes. Will you join me?

The Love Lives Here Idea

Have you decided to stick together?

Chapter 2

Our Love Story

"Every love story is beautiful, but ours is my favourite"
—Unknown Author

Every couple needs to create and own their love story. I have seen that a couple's comparisons to other people's relationships can get in the way of them creating and owning their love story.

I get it. What we see around us usually determines, to a large extent, who we are to become. We benchmark our destinations according to our environments, but if that is the standard then how do you create something of your own? How do you create something with your identity stamp if all that you do has to look or become like someone else's?

Now, you may argue that we cannot negate our environments. To this, I would agree wholeheartedly. I am not saying never look outside for inspiration or to create something magical for yourself. What I am saying is that you ought to remember something important: if you are going to create something, it must start with where you are and with what you have. Looking at other people's results does not do this for you because you never know what they did to get there.

This is like looking at your neighbour's cars and wanting to buy yourself a better model than theirs without assessing your own budget and needs. Such envy will only be to your detriment.

How does this idea apply to you and your relationship? Well, Oscar Wilde once wrote "Most people are other people. Their thoughts are someone else's opinions, their lives a mimicry, their passions a quotation." The truth is in this statement. It is sad to know that a lot of relationships I have admired never survived the challenges that broke them apart. After long heartfelt conversations with these couples, I would conclude that comparison not only steals joy but also destroys it. It robs the relationship of being something different for the couple and it destroys the relationship because the things you are looking for—whether it be from the relationship, yourself, or your partner—will never be apparent. This only leads to heartbreak and separation if not recognised much earlier.

In one of the interviews I conducted, Mrs Chisara mentioned that she compared her husband, Mr Chisara, to someone she had seen in a movie. In her mind, they would live a "happily ever after" romantic life when they moved in together. She took the movie too seriously, not knowing that movies are written to keep your attention by entertaining you with ideas. What she soon realised was that her reality was far from her movie-based fantasy. Her husband was unlike the movie character, and she resented him for not playing the part. After some heart-to-heart conversations with her husband, she eventually started coming to terms with her reality. Her husband was never going to be the same as the character in the movie. This realisation improved their relationship. They also went for counselling, and it helped them to get to the point of understanding each other for who they were. Cheekily, I guess you could say she did get her happy ending—but it had to be based on their reality.

Not all that glitters is gold. It's usually hard work

If you were to see the Chisara's now, you would want to emulate them immediately based on their current results. Remember, while it is easy to want their results, we never truly know the work it takes to get there.

Take for instance the Makhatini's. They lost their two-year-old to drowning after their second year in marriage. They blamed each other and fought over who was supposed to have been looking after the child. As if that was not enough of a painful experience to go through, the couple went through a period of financial problems after the wife lost her job. This ordeal forced the husband to become the sole breadwinner. This resulted in strain and stress for him because his salary was not enough to cover all expenses. Just think of schooling two kids, paying a mortgage and other living expenses. It's not easy. Eventually, however, the wife found a job, and this improved their circumstances. Seeing them now, you would never think that, and chances are you would never want the same path to get to their results.

The lesson here is simple. You cannot compare yourself to another couple because you never know what that couple had to go through to get there. Learn to define what you want as a couple and thereafter work towards it, not to keep up with the Joneses, but to create and maintain something that you want.

The Love Lives Here Idea

Every relationship has its challenges.

If you want to thrive as a couple, do not compare yourselves to other couples. Instead, create a safe environment where you two can communicate honestly about anything and everything.

Every love story is beautiful. Tell me, how will you make your love story your favourite?

In the next chapter, we will talk about why couples stay together. You will be surprised why they do.

Chapter 3

Why We are Still Together

"Even if we fight a lot, I still want you in my life"
—Rajendra Jain

Change is inevitable. There are two types of changes. The ones we administer, such as trying to save more money or lose weight. Then the second type of change is the one that is administered to us—COVID-19 and its implications are good examples of such changes. The difference between these two changes is that we are proactive about one of them while needing to react to the other.

As couples, sometimes we are guilty of wanting to administer changes to our partners.

Take a look at this situation:

The other day at work I ran into Bob. We chatted over lunch, and he dropped a bombshell on me. "Rodney," he said, "Becky and I are going to get a divorce." I was stunned. "Why? What happened? You two seem so happy together." "Well," he said, "ever since we got married my wife has tried to change me. She got me to stop drinking, smoking, running around at all hours at the night, she taught me how to dress well, enjoy the fine arts, gourmet cooking, classical music, and how to invest in the stock market." "Are you a little bitter because she spent so much time trying to change you?" I prompted, "Nah I'm not bitter. Now that I'm so improved, she just isn't good enough for me."

I tried to look for a joke on how men try to change women, but I was not able to find any. I doubt it means that men wouldn't try to change their wives. For example, when they get married to an independent woman, they might encourage her to be a stay-at-home wife and leave him to take care of the finances. Was this her plan? It would be one thing if she decided to change, but if that change is administered to her, and it is outside her choice, then is it fair?

Why do couples want their partner to be what they want as opposed to who they are?

From my experience and research, I found that people within relationships naturally have expectations. It is human to have expectations. These expectations come from the way we have been brought up, such as a lady or gentleman that may have had a father who was the sole breadwinner. The chances of that lady expecting her partner not to be a breadwinner are pretty slim, while on the other hand, the gentleman would believe that it is his job to be the breadwinner. The expectations these two have are not wrong and neither are they right. What may be a problem is when either of them marries someone who does not have the same expectations as them and no middle ground is pursued.

All expectations should be communicated. Especially the expectations you are conscious of. Thereafter, they should be discussed, and each should be weighted on merit and relevance. Merit in the sense that it actually does apply to the couple, and that it would enhance the relationship. Relevance in the sense that they can practically act on it.

In the example I shared, the couple should determine if it is financially viable to have a sole breadwinner. They should both have a say and reach a reasonable solution together.

This can also be applied to spiritual matters. Whether one of the individuals in a relationship believes that both should be going to church. It could also be how one of the parties believes that they should both have a workout schedule—even though only one is really into working out. Both of these expectations, I believe, are extremely healthy. What would not be healthy is when these expectations are enforced instead of being discussed.

Being proactive about knowing your partner and taking time to understand them is key. This could help in accepting who they are. In the interview, Mr and Mrs Isaac mentioned that they did not try to change each other. As a result, after their wedding, there was not much of a shift in behaviour towards each other because they already knew each other well. They understood their individual strengths and weaknesses and instead of using that information to change the other person, they used that knowledge to complement each other.

When do you realise that you have not accepted your partner for who they are?

You realise this when resentment begins to build. This resentment is built on the fact that everything they do turns out to not be good enough for you. They seem to miss the mark consistently. In my relationship, I prefer to be kissed on the forehead and to receive hugs from the back but Mr K does not do this. He had his way of showing affection and I struggled to accept it. I had a problem with him not doing what I expected, and I resented him for it. I remember how I would get moody and look for errors in him and around the home. I would even give him the silent treatment from time to time for not getting my way. Eventually, after I saw how my actions were weighing heavy on the relationship, I had to begrudgingly accept that these were my expectations, and I was trying to enforce them on him. Had I accepted him for who he was, I may have never developed the grudges I had towards him in the first place. This is the importance of accepting people for who they are as opposed to who you would prefer them to be.

How do couples accept each other for who they are?

A great place to start would be by accepting each other's weaknesses. Mr Petrus knew from the onset that Mrs Petrus was not the lady who would be in the kitchen, doing the cleaning, doing the laundry, and packing the cupboards. Fortunately, he has never minded taking care of the house. Mrs Petrus said that when she asks Mr Petrus to get water for her from the kitchen he sometimes takes up to thirty minutes to bring it. In his defence, when he sometimes gets to the kitchen, he realises that there are dishes to wash and that takes up his time.

Their story goes back to when they were still dating. While they were still dating Mrs Petrus' first visit to Mr Petrus' home was unsettling for her. She said that she saw how neat the house was and how orderly the cupboards were. She wondered why God was sending her a man who already knew how to take care of himself. She doubted whether she would be able to handle him and keep him happy. The differences did not stop them because they understood their weaknesses and strengths. If you think of it, society is very patriarchal. Women have always been expected to handle all the chores and with the modern-day city living demands, even more is expected of them, from both the home and workplace. What I like about Mr and Mrs Petrus is that they defy these societal roles and do what works for them. Your relationship should never be subjected to societal beliefs. Figure things out for yourselves and act accordingly.

I have briefly chatted to you about expectations and how they can cause problems, but sometimes expectations are meant to be held as standards and not meant to be compromised.

When shouldn't you accept your partner for who they are?

We have expectations of character and personality. There is an enormous difference between character and personality. For example, Mrs Petrus does not like house chores and that is part of her personality. Personality is about preference while a character is about morals. House chores are not a moral issue. Her character is not in question because of what she dislikes. If, however, Mrs Petrus does something unlawful, that is a moral issue, and her character may come into question. I would recommend that you have such a list with you. Take time to know when something is simply a preference versus it being unlawful. We can compromise on personality differences, but issues to do with character must be looked at carefully. Being unlawful should never be entertained nor should it be compromised.

I have a secular humanist. Mr K is not a churchgoer, but he is very respectful of my need to go to church. We have debates now and then about our different beliefs, but it remains a healthy debate. If his beliefs and the debates prevent me from practising my religion then, I am free to express myself lawfully according to the constitution of South Africa. If he forced me to not go to church, I would have found it difficult to accept him as a partner and continue with the relationship. I also think he would find this relationship difficult as we would continuously be at loggerheads.

The Love Lives Here Idea

As couples, we may want to change each other due to the expectations we have for each other or the relationship. Perhaps, the better alternative is accepting who our partners are and them accepting who we are. You can do this by understanding each other's strengths and weaknesses while strengthening the relationship with your strengths but also knowing how to cover both your shortfalls. Shortfalls that are more personality-based, and not character flaws.

What are some of your expectations? Have you discussed them with your partner?

In the next chapter, we will talk about how couples face challenges and overcome them.

Chapter 4

How to Climb the Mountains of Marriage

"Sometimes I wonder if love is worth fighting for. Then I look at you. I am ready for war."
—Wiz Khalifa

Couples face many challenges in their journey of marriage. Most of these are incorporated into financial, spiritual, mental, physical, and emotional challenges.

Let's see how some of the couples, that I interviewed, reacted to these challenges.

Financial Challenges

Mr and Mrs Jacobs shared how the pursuit of full-time ministry changed their financial circumstances. Mr Jacobs left his full-time job to pursue ministry. After some months had elapsed, it dawned on them that his salary was desperately needed for the upkeep of the family. They got into financial trouble and were no longer able to maintain the household properly. Although they had hit tough times, through fervent prayer, God kept bringing people to support them. According to the couple, just as Elijah from the Bible had been fed by ravens when he was hungry and weak, they had food and household items brought to them by different individuals.

Mrs Jacobs further mentioned that while having her meals, she would eat slowly so that she could make sure her kids were full before finishing her food. On several occasions, she would have had to share her meals with them. During this period, the couple decided that they would not fight. Although the period was tough—as many marriages lead to divorce due to financial trouble—their challenges brought them closer together, even after the repossession of Mrs Jacobs' once prized car. The decision to stick together, not argue, and work through things was of immense importance.

If you ever find yourself in such a situation—provided none of you has purposefully put the other in disrepute—sit down and have some ground rules of engagement with a plan of how you will get out of your financial turmoil.

Spiritual Challenges

While most spiritual challenges refer to conflicts over spiritual matters with God/ Higher Power, within oneself, and with other people. What you will realise with the couples below is that they had physical and emotional challenges that they faced by being spiritual. The issues faced in this realm either bring us closer to God or they take us away from Him. The results of either choice could bring couples together or could further draw them apart. Either way, the choice remains ours.

Ever thought of having children when you got married? The wish to have children was no different for Mr and Mrs Petrus.

They were told by doctors that they only had a one per cent chance of conceiving. While this caused slight pain for them, they decided to work against the doctors' disbelief and bring God into their challenge. It took eight years from the time they were diagnosed by the doctors to the day they birthed their son. Their faith allowed them to manifest their desire to have children. You can read more about their story in the book they co-authored called, *Believe Again*. Their journey has brought them closer to God, and as a result, closer to each other.

The challenge here is knowing that there is a larger force than you as a couple, and both of you rely on the fact that that force is for you and not against you. If both of you can meet on this foundation, then it would be easier to ride the storms of life.

Mental Challenges

Mental challenges emanate from the fact that there is a disparity between yourself and your partner when it comes to how you both see the world and the challenges that it comes with.

While this is sometimes an advantage in the relationship because there is a value in having different perspectives, however, this can sometimes be an obstacle when a partner cannot see or refuses to see the other's perspective. Essentially this means that they cannot connect. If they cannot connect, they cannot communicate and therefore, they cannot move forward.

There is a lady I know who met her partner in high school. During their relationship, she fell pregnant at the age of fourteen. She fell pregnant again at sixteen. They were still in school and prospects for their future began to look dim. She decided to push through and improve these prospects. She completed high school and looked for a job. In her first job, she worked as a cashier at a local retailer. She strived for more security, and she knew this could only be done by further growth. She looked for a new job and became an intern teacher. If you met her now, she may tell you of the several streams of income she has created and her recently obtained degree.

A stark contrast to how things started for her. Unfortunately, her partner and herself lost contact as you can imagine how conversations would be hard to sustain because mentally, they are worlds apart.

Physical Challenges

It has always been mentioned how your spouse's body will change over time—usually, this means gaining weight. Whether this is right or wrong is not the point here. The point that I would like to discuss is that in a relationship, there may be a partner that takes health seriously. They watch what they eat and frequently exercise. If this person begins to feel that you are not taking your health as seriously as they are, this could cause problems for the relationship.

I know of a couple on the verge of getting married. The lady takes health very seriously and has kept the same weight since she was in tertiary. The male, on the other hand, gained weight when he started his first job and continued to gain weight until he met her. She expressed how she felt about his weight and began to challenge him to lose weight, which he has. He was not forced into this choice but saw the light once she had explained the repercussions of him neglecting his health.

Health is an important facet of your marriage. Remember, you only get one body in this lifetime. I know on the altar you said you will be with them through sickness and health. How about you make good on the health by being proactive?

Emotional Challenges

Have you ever heard the words, "I don't know why this is hurting you? It is ridiculously small; we shouldn't even be talking about this."

Within every relationship, one person will care more for certain things than the other. When there is an argument between the two of you, if you care more for the subject matter being discussed, you may be viewed as more emotional. Yes, you are and that is not a terrible thing, nor should it be held against you.

The solution here is to know what your soft spots are and why they are there. It is important to communicate these to your partner. The next step is to know what your partner's soft spots are and learn to be honest yet tread softly when discussing them. Communication is key.

There is no such thing as over-communicating. Mr and Mrs Chisara once mentioned that whenever the other partner feels sad about what was said to them, they put time aside to find out what caused the sadness. This discussion may take them hours to conclude, but at the end of the day, the challenge will be resolved.

Challenges are meant to be overcome

I think it is important for couples to understand how they deal with challenges. In my relationship, I am the one who wants to attend to the matter as soon as it arises because I usually address matters when I am upset. Mr K wants to think about it and thereafter, have a decent chat. In the Jacobs household, Mr Jacobs prefers to address the matters immediately whilst Mrs Jacobs wants to cool down and address the matter later. Mr Chisara thinks things through whilst Mrs Chisara gets to the point without thinking the matters through. As you can see, couples have varied ways of dealing with matters, but they will deal with them.

Mr and Mrs Isaac's view is that you need to be mature and know that you are going to have challenges. This is the reason young couples divorce quickly because they may not yet be mature. That is why when they face a challenge they leave because they can't weather the storm. They don't know yet that people change, situations change, and people evolve. An unpleasant situation will not be bad for long, the same goes for a good situation; it will not be good for long. As a couple, we need to be on the same team. When you fight, it is not that you are against each other but rather, you are having a temporary argument and it will pass. If your love can't conquer that temporary argument and you don't remember that you are in a temporary argument, then it defines your marriage. A fight is not supposed to define your marriage, it is supposed to be a moment in your marriage. If the fight becomes the definition of your marriage, then it is problematic. Your marriage needs to be anchored on love. If that is the ruling in your relationship, then the fight is not going to last forever. It is going to grow you.

Secondly, when we fight, we need to learn to be neutral and constantly reflect on the situation. Was I wrong? Was he? Was she? Could we have handled that differently? We are quick to point fingers and quick to label the other person as wrong without looking at our contribution. We need to have a neutral mental framework and learn to pick our battles.

Is there a point when you should stop loving your partner because things are not rosy?

I am no expert on why or when you should divorce, but I do know that when you come to this point you will know what to do. My advice here, however, is that if you have not made amends to things that may have been challenging in the relationship, you will face the same circumstances again, and may not prevail. I know a couple who divorced. One of the divorcees married again, and soon thereafter, divorced again (Irvin, 2021).

The root cause of this is unresolved issues (Guardian, 2021). After some time had passed, they met up again and they rekindled their romance and remarried. Things are different now because they have resolved the issues they used to have. So, if you divorce, ensure that you resolve the underlying issues that led to the divorce so that you can start your new relationship on a new page.

The Love Lives Here Idea

Relationships come with challenges that are there to make you stronger and better. Through the challenges, you learn how to communicate, how to love and trust each other.

How will you and your partner begin to handle the challenges that you will face as a married couple?

In the next chapter, we are talking about how simple love is or can be if we are reasonable.

Chapter 5

LOVE IS SIMPLE

"Love takes off masks that we fear we cannot live without and know we cannot live within"
—James Baldwin

What is love?

I remember at work, sixteen years ago, how my colleagues would complain that I had no other stories to share except for talking about my boyfriend. That was when I had just met Mr K and in my defence, this was the honeymoon phase where he could do no wrong in my eyes. Everything about him was perfect.

Now we all know that the honeymoon phase does not last exceptionally long. The relationship soon graduates and all of a sudden you realise that the person you are with is not perfect.

This is when challenges begin. Arguments come to the surface and the contrast between who you met at the beginning of the relationship and who you are experiencing now, begins to become more emanant. Now don't get me wrong, this is perfectly natural.

Where we may falter is admitting we love someone during the honeymoon phase and once the honeymoon phase elapses and the challenges begin, we let our love for our partners go away. In your mind's eye, I want you to imagine perfection walking out with love when challenges knock on your relationship's door.

Are we meant to let love go when challenges come, or should it graduate from feelings to action? Regardless of what your partner may do (excluding abuse or bad characteristics) you graduate to making love a decision and not a whimsical concept.

When I started to get to know Mr K after the honeymoon phase, I began to learn that regardless of any imperfections, I wanted him in my life. It was in those moments that I decided to act accordingly by loving him more with my actions as opposed to my feelings.

Was this smooth sailing? You and I both know that it is not. This is when the relationship either becomes worthwhile or not and that depends on how you define love. Would you define it as a feeling or as an action?

What is Love?

The Bible gives a beautiful description of love in 1 Corinthians 13:4-8 (New International Version):

> *"Love is patient, love is kind. It does not envy, it does not boast, it is not proud. It does not dishonor others, it is not self-seeking, it is not easily angered, it keeps no record of wrongs. Love does not delight in evil but rejoices with the truth. It always protects, always trusts, always hopes, always perseveres. Love never fails. But*

where there are prophecies, they will cease; where there are tongues they will be stilled; where there is knowledge, it will pass away."

The Bible outlines that love is a decision and I have allowed this to be the foundation of how I treat Mr K. Love was interpreted differently by the people I interviewed. I would like to share some of these with you in hopes that you will find your definition amongst them.

As I sat with Mr Makhathini, he mentioned that loving someone is knowing that you can take your heart out, leave it there for the entire day and you will find it intact when you return. His wife agreed with this and mentioned how love is having a person you trust always be there for you. Within these two definitions, we find that love is the ability to be vulnerable while trusting that your vulnerability will never leave you in a worse off position. Vulnerability breeds an abundance of trust.

Mr and Mrs Jones defined love as comprising of shared experiences which, when you look back on them, you long for more moments like those in the future. It's looking back at spots you visited and having that warm feeling fill your body and then having faith that there is more for you to share.

I am not too sure how you felt as you read the different interpretations, but it does show how love can mean different things to different people. No matter how different they are – happiness, a sense of comfort, deep care, and looking forward to a great future seem to flow through. You will notice that none of the couples looks at love as a flimsy or whimsical feeling. It requires that both parties make love as solid as a rock. Love should have a sense of permanence.

If love can be this simple, what makes it so complicated at times?

What makes love complicated?

Even though love is simple, what complicates it is the fact that two humans are expressing it to each other. There are days I love to be loving and there are days that I don't. I am sure you feel the same way sometimes. It is during these times—when you feel not so loving and when you don't want to be so kind—that you realise that love can be complicated.

Apart from how you may feel on a day, there is the fact that you are not perfect. There will be days when your partner does something and right after they have done it, when you could have met them with grace, you stoop low. Instead of being mature and trying to get ahead by being understanding and reconnecting with your partner, the preference of an eye for an eye feels like the better alternative. In these low moments, it is not that you love your partner less or that they love you less. It is the fact that our partners are human and so are you.

During those moments of reconciliation, don't be hard on yourself or your partner. I believe that grace should be administered in these moments as it could breathe a new gust of wind into your relationship's sails. Be generous with understanding each other and be willing to compromise more.

Will this be easy? No. It is, however, worth trying because as you do so, your relationship only grows.

The Love Lives Here Idea

Love is the basis of all relationships. For this foundation to work, both of you must agree on how you will define love within your relationship. I hope that you will define it more as an action than a feeling. I hope that you will realise that while your definition of love may be perfect, you aren't, and neither is your partner. In those moments though, learn to dispense even more love.

What is your definition of love?

In the next chapter, you will learn how to be yourself and still love and respect your partner.

Chapter 6

I AM MYSELF

"Be you. The world will adjust."
—Unknown

Are you meant to be yourself in a marriage?

Both yes and no. Take a look at what the interviewees had to say.

Mr Makhathini mentioned that in marriage you have to compromise. We would all like to be ourselves at all times, but we can't. We can't because we are not married to ourselves; we are married to another person and that person may need a better version of ourselves. The fact that you have a partner that you decided to spend your life with, means you ought to consider your partner too. It is this consideration that makes us all better partners. He mentioned that he is a quiet person but knows that his wife sometimes wants to have conversations about the events that occurred during her day. While he would prefer to sit in their bedroom alone, he knows that when she needs him, he has to avail himself.

He is not advising that we become different people altogether as individuals. He is advising that we become accommodative to the person we choose to spend the rest of our lives with.

Mrs Makhathini said that she made peace with the fact that she has a lot of energy that needs to be burned. So, she does things that help her burn the energy. She is a member of Toastmasters, does outreach programmes, and organises events to use her energy. This, in turn, helps her not use her excessive energy on her husband. This helps her husband to have and enjoy his quiet moments. This is her way of being accommodative.

Mr and Mrs Petrus are completely different people even though they do everything together. Their personalities are quite different.

"I celebrate her uniqueness. I am sure if she was married to someone else, they were going to be intimidated by her because she is a strong person and she knows what she wants. I support and embrace that. I leverage that because it helps keep my focus," Mr Petrus commented. "I am not an extremely focused person on everyday things. If I need to focus on something that I am passionate about, I am super focused. On the other things, Mrs Petrus will remind me and keep me accountable. If she wasn't in my life, I would have just ignored the other small things."

Mrs Petrus shares that Mr Petrus is very disciplined; he will go to the gym in the morning at 6 o'clock. "He has lots of wisdom and I leverage that too. I am a microwave person: I want everything now. I don't want to wait for it, whereas he believes in the process, and for the process to work for us. We are completely different in our outlook on life, the way we pack our cupboards. His is in order and mine is just rolled up and thrown in but we have learned to live with each other. I remember when I went over to his house, I saw his cupboards and I laughed, and I asked God if he was sure that I should marry him because he was too orderly, and I knew that I was upside down. But here we are, and it worked."

There are two options here. You could either be accommodative of your partner like the Makhatinis, or you could leverage each other's strengths like the Petrus family. I would advise that you do both—be accommodative of each other while also learning to leverage one another's strengths.

Why people tend to not want to be themselves is marriage

If you do not know yourself then the pressure will be high for you to change yourself. This is because you have no basis to guide your thoughts, actions, and beliefs. If you are to meet someone that knows themselves, chances are high that you will dance to the rhythm of their beat. When you meet someone who doesn't know themselves, and you know yourself, it is up to you to be patient with the other person as they develop.

When both of you do not know yourselves, as in your likes and dislikes, then there is bliss, but this bliss is based on ignorance because eventually, you would both have to discover who you are and how you will interact with the newly found information about yourselves. I would recommend that if you both do not know who you are, don't get married yet. Figure out who you are so that you can be compatible within the marriage.

The ideal situation here is that both of you know yourselves and in doing so, you can become one. The idea is that both of you are two pieces of a puzzle understanding each other's grooves and sharp corners. This knowledge would allow you to build a beautiful picture of marriage.

The other factor that contributes to pressure in the relationship is family (in-laws). Sometimes they might have preconceived expectations of how a makoti (daughter-in-law) or mokgwenyane (son-in-law) should behave.

A good friend mentioned how her in-laws expect her to run around for them when they visit. They do not consider that she goes to work like her husband. Their inconsideration is peppered with unwelcome comments such as, "She doesn't even dress well. She doesn't cook on time for her husband." On the husband's side, the in-laws expect him to spend money on them at the family gatherings. If he doesn't, he is regarded as stingy. These are unnecessary pressures that we need to learn to ignore and focus on what makes us and our partners happy.

In terms of the solution to that problem, my advice is to speak to each other's families together. Do not let the pressures of your family weigh a burden on you.

How to live out your individuality within a marriage

Most couples don't work together, may not go to the same church, or always go to parties together. These are some of the things that allow them to enjoy being themselves. This time apart is known as "me time." This is important for both women and men as you don't always want to be with your partner.

Opting for "me time" is not you giving your partner the silent treatment. It's about you recharging and engaging in activities that are particularly interesting to you. My "me time" is attending Toastmasters meetings and Mr K's "me time" is watching some documentaries or reading a newspaper. "Me time" eventually rejuvenates each person so that they can add more to experiences enjoyed together.

Not all couples believe in "me time" and that's fine. The point is that you know whether this applies to you or not. If it does, then certainly use it and be respectful of that as well.

Individual vs Together

We are born as individuals, even twins are individuals, getting married doesn't necessarily mean that one must forget who they are and conform. In marriage, we do not change who we are, but we accommodate each other. Mr Jacobs said, during the interview, "What makes me think that when we get married, I can start telling my wife that what she has been doing all her life is wrong? She survived all these years without me and all of a sudden how she was living is wrong?" We do not get married to change one another but to be each other's companions.

Mrs Jacobs mentioned that one's partner should not be their "happiness" partner. Her views were, "I think that when one depends on the other person to make them happy they are setting themselves up for failure. You should know that your partner is not your happiness keeper. Your partner is your companion. Being happy means doing things that fulfil you, that develop and grow you or rather you should know where your happiness lies. I know that my happiness does not lie around my husband, my work, and other stuff. My happiness depends on my developing, my helping others, and my knowing that my kids are growing healthily. That's where my happiness comes from. So, once I know that I fulfilled those trivial things then I can say I am happy. You need to know what makes you happy."

She goes on to say, "let's maybe define that happiness as when you know that you can sleep at night without having worries, even if you don't have food in your house and you know that the following day would be better. Once you know that you are content even without putting too much pressure on your partner." Know that they are also human and also have their challenges in life and you are there to support each other and not to bring each other down.

The Love Lives Here Idea

There is nothing wrong with being different. That is what attracted you to each other. What you must work on is how to become more compatible. This means being accommodative of each other. It is that accommodation that brings the two of you to become one.

How will you remain an individual but seek to grow as one?

In the next chapter, I will share how you can make your love beautiful and be able to withstand tough times.

Chapter 7

LOVE IS BEAUTIFUL

"Every heart sings a song, incomplete until another heart whispers back. Those who wish to sing always find a song."
—Plato

Is love always beautiful?

Love is beautiful, but the relationship may not always be. The beauty tends to fade when the relationship moves past the honeymoon phase. The honeymoon phase is characterised by four things according to an article I read by Dr Jessica Higgins (Higgins, 2021). The first is that during the first eighteen months of this relationship, the couple does not see any flaws in each other. To them, they are perfect in every regard. The second thing they do is assume that they have everything in common and believe they have no differences, which after eighteen months, they figure out is not the case. The third characteristic is that they give and receive willingly with no reservations. The fourth characteristic is that this is an important phase in the relationship because, without it, the couple never actually bonds. The point I am making is not that this phase is good or bad, I am simply ensuring you understand it for what it truly is—a passing phase and not a moment in perpetuity. In a relationship, a woman wants to be loved and appreciated and the man wants to be respected. If both men and women don't get what they ask for, then love fades over time.

The other phases of a relationship directly after the honeymoon phase are the power struggle, stability, commitment, and the co-creation phase.

The power struggle phase is characterised by seeing the flaws in one another and realising that you are not the same. I believe this is when most couples have to decide on whether they will remain together or whether they will fall apart.

The stability phase is characterised by the realisation and acceptance that you are different, and you seek not to change your partner. Mr and Mrs Isaac exude this well concerning how they pray. They do not pray together, instead, Mrs Isaac prays in her bedroom and Mr Isaac prays in the car while driving to work. They have accepted that they pray differently and would want to express that as well.

The fourth phase is the commitment phase which is characterised by finding the balance between individuality and being together. This is where things like "me time" and time together become a theme.

The last phase is the co-creation phase, which is characterised by the couple understanding that they can do more together. Only fifteen per cent of couples reach this phase. In this phase, the couple focuses on the collective effect of working as a team. The couple works towards deepening their connection and intimacy. In this phase, the couple can achieve greater goals with their combined effort and usually work on collaborative projects where they make contributions to the world beyond their partnership.

Mr and Mrs Jacobs are the epitome of co-creation. They run a church together and are part of the same Toastmasters club. Whatever one does, the other participates as well. They have discovered how they can do more when they are together. Mr and Mrs Petrus co-authored a book called *Believe Again*. The Mjilas run several businesses together and the Joneses attend personal development courses together and also run some of their businesses together. They also fall into this category.

It is important to understand that the individuals within a couple can be at distinct phases and the point is to know where you are and then know where your partner is and begin to build a bridge to whoever is at a higher phase.

How to make love beautiful

Apart from knowing which phase you two may be in as a couple, what makes love beautiful is navigating through the distinct phases.

Think about all the stories you could tell by navigating through all these phases. Look back at how you triumphed in these phases and gain confidence as you look at the marriage that you two are building. As you navigate the phases, you grow stronger as a couple.

The Love Lives Here Idea

Love is beautiful, but what makes it beautiful is the journey both of you take on in making the relationship formidable. As you do so, the memories you create will build the confidence that you will both have for your future.

How will you make your marriage beautiful?

In the next chapter, I will share with you how you can, and should, love unconditionally.

Chapter 8

WHAT IS UNCONDITIONAL LOVE?

"If it does not challenge you, it will not change you"
— Fres DeVito

Mrs Makhathini said the only unconditional love that exists is between God and His people, and between parents and their children. In marriage, love is something we choose. You've loved so many people, but it doesn't mean you wanted to marry all of them. Marriage is like another career; you have to work at it for it to work. There are things to work on, for example, your partner might not like kissing you before they brush their teeth and you, on the other hand, may not mind. They end up accommodating you and become comfortable with kissing before they brush their teeth. Love is not superficial, it is never about what you look like or how you are dressed, it's about the value that you see in each other. Love only works when you realise that marriage is one's true career. People change jobs all the time, but you can't do the same with marriage. You are in it for the long haul. In our house, we say, "I love you forever in seven days" which means that as long as a week has seven days, our love will remain.

Mr Petrus feels that love is a decision. When they had their journey with infertility, the decision was, "I am not going to change the way I feel about her because we've now hit this hurdle or speed hump on the road. Even when life comes at you and circumstances have changed, because it is the decision that I made, I can just go with it." To give an example, like Mrs Petrus said that I am very disciplined in going to the gym and watching what I eat. I have that kind of approach with everything, even when it comes to love. It is a decision that I made so that is how it is going to be.

Mrs Petrus views unconditional love as accepting everything about the person—their strengths and weaknesses, the things that irritate you and the things that make you happy. It is just accepting the person. Love the person for who they are and the package that they come in.

Mrs Jones sees it as loving the next person even if they are doing "something wrong," or something to hurt you. You love them no matter what. Mr Jones views it as jumping into a raging ocean or burning fire to rescue the next person. Trying to save your partner in a demanding situation.

Mr Chisara highlights that it is not holding things against each other. Accept them as they are. Allow them to be who they are and love them as they are. When you are still in the initial stages of the relationship, you'd think that the person is just too beautiful that going to the toilet does not suit them. Unconditional love is knowing that they do go to the toilet but love them regardless of the smell they leave.

Mrs Chisara states that one should know that they have flaws and accept them as they are. Have the heart to see your partner grow. You put your partner first before yourself, you want them to grow and become a better version of themselves. You sacrifice what you need, to be a better person.

Love is unconditional but it starts with conditions

While love is unconditional, the truth is that it starts with conditions. These conditions are the standards you set before your get married. Things like the commandments and your obedience to them.

I say this because if you marry someone who does not live up to your standards, and I mean reasonable standards, then it is hard to love them. After all, they will contravene your standards daily.

An example of this could be a car that uses petrol. That is the car's condition, and as long as it is full it will go anywhere and everywhere you want it to. If, however, you fill the tank with anything but petrol, say water, it doesn't matter how hard you pray for the car to move, it will remain still. The same with unconditional love, for it to thrive it must live in the confines of conditions.

Now you may ask, "But doesn't that contradict everything you have just said Gadi?" No, it doesn't. Remember that marrying your partner was a choice and as long as there is a choice, then conditions need to be met. Once the conditions are met, then unconditional love can abound.

The Love Lives Here Idea

Love should be unconditional, but for it to be unconditional it has to be met with conditions.

What are your conditions? Are they reasonable? More importantly, have you discussed and mutually agreed on them?

In the next chapter, I will share with you how to spot a cheater and what to do when you spot them.

Chapter 9

CHEATING

"Cheating is a choice, not a mistake."
—Unknown

What is cheating?

Withholding information from your partner as well as doing things that you know your partner would not approve of. Your partner's approval in this context means doing inappropriate things and things that would harm the relationship. If it is a secret that you are keeping from your partner, then it might not be something your partner would approve of.

Defining cheating becomes complex because there are diverse types of relationships whose limits and boundaries could be differently defined. What some individuals view as cheating, others may view as a normal part of the relationship. Some people may view cheating as being purely physical whilst others may feel betrayed by emotional cheating. In an article on Fatherly.com titled, "What, Exactly, Counts as Cheating?" Rick Clemons, a Life Coach, mentions that some of his clients realised that infidelity came from a space of being misaligned with their own values. Something in their current relationship isn't in alignment with their values so they go seeking it elsewhere and then get caught up in an affair (Simons, 2021).

Our views of what may be okay in a relationship can stem from how we were socialised—the stories we heard growing up, our family dynamics, cultural expectations, advice from elders, or the media we consume. The people we meet may have a different worldview to ours and may not see cheating in the same light we do. This lends itself to a big conflict within the relationship as there is a mismatch of ideals. The people in the relationship need to define it for themselves.

Why do people cheat?

Cheating is one of the main reasons for breakups. It has been argued that men cheat more than women, that argument according to the online article, "When a Partner Cheats" on NY Times website. Jane E. Brody mentions that fifteen per cent of married women have had extramarital affairs whereas that percentage increases by ten per cent when it comes to men. Some men have disputed the claim by saying that women are simply good at hiding their cheating. There are several reasons why people cheat, and it only takes the guilty party to open up and tell it all. Unfortunately, the truth rarely comes out because many take the defensive approach to protect themselves.

Speaking on Eusebius McKaiser's show 702 (radio station) on 13 April 2019, renowned sexologist Dr Eve mentioned that to some people, cheating could be a way of spicing up a dull relationship. In my research, I found that sometimes women cheat because they want to boost their confidence. One of the interviewees said that when she cheated, it was because she did not feel beautiful and wanted her old self back. It is quite common for women to feel unpretty and unappreciated. As women grow, their bodies change. Age, work, and family life, in general, wears them down. Physically, they are no longer the same young woman you asked out back then, but the love of attention and compliments never goes away. Not getting this from their partner is dangerous territory for the relationship. If someone else can ignite that spark by making them feel more appreciated, the possibility of cheating increases. That being said, one's bubble of confidence should never depend on other people's approval because if you do not get it from your partner, you may end up opening gates of destruction.

Why Men Cheat

Men will most likely cheat for the same reasons that women may cheat. In some instances, they even bet that they could get a certain girl. If a man grew up not getting attention from girls or women, they can easily get over-excited and pursue sexual adventures.

Sometimes men also cheat because they do not express their emotions to their partners. Ms Maart's ex-husband cheated on her after they had lost their second son. His solution for escaping the pain was cheating. She was mourning the loss of their son and went through major depression. He chose to confide in a female colleague and that went a little overboard. They got too close until they ended up in a romantic relationship. It is also fair to say that society has, to some degree, given men the freedom to cheat and get away with little or no consequence. This is one of the reasons why men can cheat, have kids out of wedlock, and still face no consequences. If culture permits, they might even bring in a sister wife.

Revenge can also be one of the reasons that people cheat. Either men or women could fall under this category. This is simply because they were hurt and now, they seek vengeance. While it is understandable, I think it is important to highlight that revenge may even the playing field initially but in the end, you will only hurt yourself in doing so.

How do you recognise a cheater?

Some common tell-tale signs that a cheater displays include personality changes, particularly if cheating is not something that they are used to. They might have mood swings, erratic behaviour, and make an increased effort in their grooming. Ms Maart said that the other way you can recognise a cheater is in changes in their spending patterns. Your partner may start spending more than he or she usually does. They buy things that never get home, for example, if you have access to their transactional history, you will see flowers, perfumes, colognes et cetera. Cheaters may start telling lies and spend more time away from home. Sometimes they would pick a fight as a way of getting out of the house.

How do you recognise that you might cheat?

There is no one size fits all approach, but there are a lot of commonalities. You should never accept a message you would not allow your partner to read. When you feel the need to delete a particular message, whether the message is innocent or not, that is a red flag. This might be an innocent act of protecting your partner, but it can be viewed as cheating. Some couples have rules such as not reading each other's messages unless permitted to do so. This is done out of trust.

How to come clean after cheating

Ms Maart believes that if you know that you are sorry for what you did then don't come clean—it will only cause trouble in your marriage. She is talking from experience. She said that she only cheated when she and her ex-husband were dating. So, one day after an exceptionally long time in their marriage, they had a honeymoon phase and were talking about anything and everything. She then confessed the cheating to her husband and things turned ugly. Even though the husband cheated twice with the same person whilst they were married, the tables turned, and he made it seem as though the challenges in the marriage were her fault. In her opinion, don't come clean if it was a mistake and you promise yourself to never do it again, but bear in mind, cheating is not a mistake, it is a choice. She said that sometimes if the partner confesses, it can lead to a devastating heartbreak. If the partner mentions the name of the hotel where they slept, whenever you pass there, hear, or see the name, it will remind you of the confession or worse, you would always imagine what could have happened when they were in there.

Another option for rebuilding the relationship after cheating includes working with a marriage counsellor. They could help you express your hurt and work through secrets that may break the relationship if not resolved. Counselling could help you communicate in a healthier way to get to the root of your challenges. This could be a lengthy process which may also be emotionally draining. You must only choose this option if you are both willing to make it work, otherwise, it would be a futile attempt.

The Love Lives Here Idea

Cheating will hurt the relationship.

How will you and your partner address cheating and try to circumvent it?

Chapter 10

WHAT THE INTERVIEWED COUPLES WISHED I ASKED

"The art and science of asking questions is the source of all knowledge."
—Thomas Berger

You are in for a treat as this chapter was birthed from not following the script. In this chapter, the couples share extra nuggets that would aid you along your journey of marriage. The themes shared in this chapter include more information on sex, tips on pre-marital counselling, and how to deal with empty nest syndrome. Enjoy.

Mr and Mrs Makhathini share their views on intimacy, goal setting, and marriage counselling.

The importance of intimacy and sexual relationship is crucial to marriage. You are not siblings. You might find other people attractive, and that's normal, but you should know what you have at home. Sex and intimacy are important. They must both be there as they are at the core of the relationship. When we talk about intimacy, it shouldn't be about just getting into the bedroom. You need to keep up. "Your kids and anyone who knows you should know that you guys love each other. There is this myth that Black people don't kiss or hug when around people. Those who know us, know that when we see each other, we give each other a hug and a kiss when we greet each other. Kids should see a lot of that. This also serves as foreplay before you get to the bedroom."

"When we entered into marriage, we were not young. We loved each other. Our hearts were jumping up and down. The heart is important in marriage, but so is the mind. I always think of the impact we could have had if we had set marriage goals and reviewed the goals closer to the time. Running a marriage like a business could be very fulfilling because you would be reaching goals. I think we faltered along the way because we didn't set any goals. This could have helped us achieve quite a lot because we would know where we failed, and we would work on those areas. Newlyweds could consider adopting this mentality of setting goals for their marriage. Things get tougher as you grow. Kids grow up, the house becomes smaller, and cars need to be upgraded. The wise thing to do would be to take care of that business from the day it is started. You won't master it as you go, you must have a plan, set goals, and stick to them."

Last words from the wife. "People should go to marriage counselling because these services are available. This puts you in a better position as a couple and allows you to discuss your plans. Maybe he has a plan of having children after three years and you are planning to have them after five years. This needs to be discussed. Pre-marital counselling is something people need to consider. When the going gets tough, I always remember 1 Corinthians 13:4-8, 'love is patient, love is kind.' When you are upset with your partner and you read that verse, you will find something that will inspire you."

Mr and Mrs Jones speak about the empty nest syndrome and how their parents' relationships influenced their lives

"When our children were gone, and we were facing an empty nest, we sat down and discussed what we could do that was a shared interest. We felt that it was important to reconnect because we had spent all these years raising children and dealing with the rush and hecticness of life. We decided it was good to have something that we both loved and enjoyed. It was great that we did that. We went to a game ranger course that lasted for a year. Lots of things have happened because of that." It was great to do something that we both loved and hadn't done before. It was worthwhile. It gives you something to talk about because couples often find themselves talking about their children.

Everything that everyone does, comes from somewhere. How did your parents' relationship impact you? How did you deal with that? For Mrs Jones, her father locked the house at night. He went all around the house and locked all the doors, the garage, and the gate. In Mr Jones' house, his mom did that. At the beginning of their marriage, it was quite tough. Mrs Jones never got up to lock the house because she expected Mr Jones to do it, but he expected her to do it. It took them a while to figure that one out. They made it their collective responsibility.

Mr Jones' mom, who is now seventy-eight years old, recently got married. His parents got divorced after twenty-five years of marriage. Her mother's new marriage is filled with constant fighting. They are rude to each other and live in the UK. When looking at this relationship, Mr Jones learned that you don't want to marry someone for the wrong reasons.

In Mrs Jones' case, her mother was hands-on and did everything for her children. Mrs

Jones realises that she took on this habit. "If we were ever going away and I had to leave my children, it would always be with my mother because I knew she would take good care of them. We never really wanted to leave them with Mr Jones' mother because I don't think that she liked children."

Mr and Mrs Chisara discuss how sex could add value to a marriage

How does sex add value in marriage? Mr Chisara says it should be enjoyed. "People think that sex is only enjoyable when stealing it, but I think that you must constantly have it. Show each other your emotions. During sex, that's when you become one. You can't hide when you are intimate. You are receiving and they are taking something away from you. What makes sex boring is when couples take it for granted. When you get used to each other, it becomes important to continue to spice things up. After three months of our marriage, we both didn't know how to have sex. When we look back at what we used to do, we laugh and ask ourselves what on earth were we doing?

Until we discovered ourselves. We used to think that it should be like in the movies. They always show fast-paced scenes. We were never getting satisfied. We then decided to be nice, gentle, and slow. That day changed everything. Don't neglect your sex life. When we have an argument or heart to heart conversation, we seal the deal with good sex."

Mr and Mrs Petrus shed light on why marriages break down

"During our pre-marital counselling sessions, our pastor touched on three things that build and break marriages. They are finance, sex, and communication. If you build on these three things, you will have a solid marriage. There is a song that says, 'no romance without finance.' It becomes exceedingly difficult to romance when there is no finance. The romance goes out of the window because you are financially stressed. You forsake the element of intimacy, which is extremely important in marriage. Intimacy is not just a physical act; it is a spiritual act as well. It bonds people in a way that is not just physical. It is what makes a marriage because it was made for marriage. When people bond in this way, there is just this intimacy that you end up knowing each other's thoughts. When you are intimate with one another, you become one. The more the sex, the more the oneness, the more agreement, the more things gel. When that gets pulled apart in a marriage, that is often when the problems start."

Mr Petrus speaks about vulnerability. "Vulnerability is something that you can build on. Sometimes you wonder how others live together because there are too many secrets between them. If you are a friend of someone in this situation, you tend to hear all the secrets that their partner knows nothing about. I had a colleague who was on a fertility journey alone without her husband. She was going for doctors' visits, procedures, and tests whilst hiding her feelings from her husband. When she found out that she was pregnant, she didn't tell her husband. She had a fear of having another miscarriage and did not want to disappoint him. I think we need to be vulnerable with each other. I have seen couples that are just not real with each other. It is like they are wearing masks around each other. I often advised this colleague to let her husband in on her thoughts and feelings, she might have been surprised by his reaction. In some instances, one of the partners would use large sums of money without the knowledge of the other partner. When things are hidden from each other it indicates that something is wrong. If you can be vulnerable with each other, and cry in front of each other, you will be able to go through everything. You won't feel the need to pretend around each other and hide things. You won't have to do things on your own. I also think that this is an opportunity for a third person to come into your marriage. If you are not being vulnerable with your partner, then who are you being vulnerable with? That is how bonds are created with third parties because you are now connecting on an emotional level with someone else. That space should be for your husband or wife."

The Love Lives Here Idea

While the advice here was not asked for in my initial set of questions, the content here still blew my mind. The lessons I gathered from these couples reminded me that there will always be an extra mile worth covering. You never come to the end of the road, there is still more worth doing. So, in that same breath, I challenge you to use this book as the starting material to strengthen your relationship as opposed to the only solution for your marriage.

How do you plan on improving your relationship after reading this book?

About the Author

Gadifele grew up not knowing what she wanted in life. She had no confidence and no life plan. She then met Mr K, her husband, and they had kids. Even with a loving husband and adorable children, Gadifele still had no confidence or a life plan.

She joined Toastmasters in 2016 and things took a turn for the better. She learned how to prepare and present speeches. The feedback she received from her evaluators helped her gain confidence. She channelled her newly found confidence and became a businesswoman. Currently, Gadi owns two businesses, is a student for life, and believes that without courage and confidence one cannot make it in this world.

She is also a relationship coach, who coaches couples on pragmatic ways to improve communication with each other. She equips couples with problem-solving techniques that ensure they deal with their challenges effectively.

She holds the highest accolade in Toastmasters, Distinguished Toastmaster (DTM). She has a Diploma in Marketing and is looking forward to writing and publishing her second book in the "...Lives Here" series.

Soon Gadi aims to obtain the accolade, "Businesswoman of the year" and will one day do her PhD.

If you want to reach out to her, you can do so at the following email addresses.

gadi@gadmo.co.za
For home or office cleaning services

info@futureleadersza.co.za
For Impactful Future Leaders.
We teach kids (ten to seventeen-years-old) public speaking, communication, and leadership skills that improve their self-confidence.

gadispeaks@exclusivemail.co.za
For relationship coaching and speaking engagements

She looks forward to hearing from you.

Books to Watch Out For in the Future:

1. Money Lives Here
2. Leadership Lives Here

REFERENCES

Brody, B.F, (2018, January 22). The New York Times. Retrieved from When a Partner Cheats: https://www.nytimes.com/2018/01/22/well/marriage-cheating-infidelity.html

Collins, M. (2020, 12 05). *Positive Psychology*. Retrieved from Positive Psychology: https://positivepsychology.com/communication-in-relationships/#improve-communication-relationships

Eggerichs, D. E. (2004). Love and Respect. In D. E. Eggerichs, *Love and Respect*.

Guardian, T. (2021, January 09). *The Guardian*. Retrieved from https://www.theguardian.com/lifeandstyle/2019/aug/13/second-chance-first-love-meet- couples-marry-divorce-remarry

Higgins, J. (2021, January 10). What Does The Development of Intimacy Look Like In

Relationship? Retrieved from https://drjessicahiggins.com/what-does-the-development-of-intimacy-look-like-in-relationship/

Irvin, M. (2021, January 09). *32 Shocking Divorce Statistics*. Retrieved from https://www.mckinleyirvin.com/family-law-blog/2012/october/32-shocking-divorce-statistics/

Lober, J. (2014). The 5 Stages of a Relationship and How to Keep Yours Strong. Retrieved 17 January 2021 from https://www.parentmap.com/article/the-5-stages-of-a-relationship-and-how-to-keep-yours-strong

Simons, S. (2021, September 1). Fatherly.com. Retrieved March 2022, from What, Exactly, Counts As Cheating?: https://www.fatherly.com/love-money/what-counts-as-cheating/

www.ingramcontent.com/pod-product-compliance
Lightning Source LLC
Chambersburg PA
CBHW030852090426
42737CB00009B/1195

9780620916752